40 days
Encounter with the Lord

40 days

Encounter *with the* Lord

Nethlie Jinius

XULON PRESS

Xulon Press
555 Winderley Pl, Suite 225
Maitland, FL 32751
407.339.4217
www.xulonpress.com

© 2023 by Nethlie Jinius

All rights reserved solely by the author. The author guarantees all contents are original and do not infringe upon the legal rights of any other person or work. No part of this book may be reproduced in any form without the permission of the author.

Due to the changing nature of the Internet, if there are any web addresses, links, or URLs included in this manuscript, these may have been altered and may no longer be accessible. The views and opinions shared in this book belong solely to the author and do not necessarily reflect those of the publisher. The publisher therefore disclaims responsibility for the views or opinions expressed within the work.

Unless otherwise indicated, Scripture quotations taken from the King James Version (KJV)–*public domain*.

Unless otherwise indicated, Scripture quotations taken from the Holy Bible, New International Version (NIV). Copyright © 1973, 1978, 1984, 2011 by Biblica, Inc.™. Used by permission. All rights reserved.

Unless otherwise indicated, Scripture quotations taken from The Message (MSG). Copyright © 1993, 1994, 1995, 1996, 2000, 2001, 2002. Used by permission of NavPress Publishing Group. Used by permission. All rights reserved.

Paperback ISBN-13: 978-1-66288-840-3
Ebook ISBN-13: 978-1-66288-841-0

ACKNOWLEDGMENT

I thank the Lord God, Jesus, and the Holy Spirit for being the main reason why I am alive to worship and honor Him, and I thank Him for being in my team; my aspiration, and inspiration to do great things in life: I thank Him as my lover, my closest friend, my comforter, my counselor. I give God praise for my birth mother Azelia Simeon, who encourages me to be myself, and for my children, Daphney L Pierre and Nathin L Pierre who both encourage me daily to write and do great things in life. They are my pride and joy. They are the ones who say, 'Mom don't just say it, but do it.' I praise God for my niece Jennifere Jinius who believes in my dreams and supports them; my grandnephew, King N Jinius, who is my little gift from heaven; my stepnephew, Qundarius Mackey who helped with this project; my brother, Jacques Jinius, my cousin Joshue Joseph, Adely Joseph, Immacula Jean, Nezia Jean, Julien Jean, Willy Valcin and my cousin, Nerlande Charles, who stood by me at a difficult time in my life.

    I give God praise for Sandra Pierre, and Johnly Charles. My aunt Louicilia Joseph and Archil Joseph, My spiritual mothers, Dr. Jane Chrouch, Dr. Mireille Michel Simon, Pastor Joceline Bouchette, and Joyce Myer. I thank God for my sister in the Lord, Natasha Nelson, who gave me this word of knowledge years ago that God will use my writings and my life story to save people's lives and transform them. I give God praise for my friends from Beach High, Audegyne Thomas, Stephanie Voltaire, Anabella Moise, Carline Lima, Marline, and all the others; you know who you are. I give God praise for President William Jefferson Clinton; thank you Sir for answering my requests when I was a teenager in high school. For Ms. Oprah Winfrey who contributed to my future in a unique way. To my spiritual children, I love you dearly. I am also grateful for Pastor Maxime Joseph who came to evangelist in my college campus; I give thanks to God for Bishop Sterling

Joseph, Pastor Henry Fish, Pastor Francis Meristal, Pastor Malory Laurent, Pastor Phill Mercidieu, Pastor Laurent Pierre Andre, and my big brother in the Lord.

    I give God praise for Pastor Alex and Darling La Croix, Sister Wideline Romelus. Brother Leon and Lucie Pierrette. My TBN family, God bless you. Some of my heroes in the faith: TD Jakes, Joyce Myer, Prophetess Juanita Bynum, Brother Kenneth, and Gloria Copeland. I give God praise also for Jerry Savelle, my BHI Family, Pastor Benny Hinn, and staff who took the time during covid-19 to have classes via zoom. Thank you for taking the time to minister and to form fellowship with us during a time of crisis and great fear. I give God praise for my Halehem sisters in the Lord; you are the best. To my HLG family, thank you for everything. I learned a lot from you and am still learning. I give God praise for my Life Christian family, thank you. Then I give God praise for Pastor Daniel and sister Eve Gualteri, Brother Dennis, and the faculty and staff who took the proper time to educate us through divine doctrine. I give God praise for Pastor Jean Glergeau and Rosemarie Glergeau, Pastor Onondieu Chere Frere and wife. Finally, I give God praise for Brother Jean Mark and Sister Linda Charles. Thank you to the Body of Christ, my dear brothers and sisters in Hollywood and in the world, Jesus truly loves you so do I.

INTRODUCTION

Recently, I had this bright idea to collectively connect some of the generals in faith and in the body of Christ through writing. I was on a twenty-one-day Daniel fast and, every day, I fellowshipped with the Father, the Son, and the Holy Spirit. I received fresh manna from above. I decided to do a devotional with the information that I received from God. I felt led in my heart to translate a few of my spiritual mother, Dr. Mireille Michel Simon, messages from French and Creole to English; well just few of them. She loved to preach and teach the Word of God. She was a woman of God who was full of zeal and on fire for the Lord during the time she was sick, so I waited a while for the right time to tell her. Few months ago, I went to see her but I didn't know at the time that she would depart from this world to the Lord's Kingdom a month later. I told her about this project and asked her to fix it for me before I send it to the publishing company to edit since it was very messy and unorganized. She asked me to have one or two people to look at it and then she would do the final corrections.

This devotional represents a few of our generals in the faith and my fathers and mothers away from home who influenced my life; the truth is many of them I will probably never meet face to face in this lifetime. I strongly believe that waking up daily should not be taken lightly. We must give our Creator the first of everything, that includes talking to him daily, just like we do with our husbands, wives, children, family, classmates, co-workers, friends etc. It does not take one hour to communicate with God, instead start with 5 minutes; this book is a perfect beginning for you to do so. Every great man and woman of God who has spent hours seeking God's face has started somewhere at the bottom and worked their way up. The goal is to draw you near to your heavenly Father who is so patiently longing and waiting to hear from you. God is not interested in your weakness, your past failures, or your mistakes. He is in you. You are His most valuable creation. He genuinely believes that you are his greatest achievement even though we wound him every day.

Bibliography

DR. Mireille Michelle Simon, Kenneth and Gloria Copeland, John G lake, TD Jakes, few of my notes from Life Christian University, Pastor Benny Hinn. The Holy Bible NIV AND KING JAMES version, The message Bible, The Vines complete Expository Dictionary, THE NEW STRONG'S CONCISE CONCORDANCE AND VINE'S CONCISE DICTIONARY OF THE BIBLE.

Day 1

The Christ In You

The word Christ means: Christos anointed, Messiah.

The single title, Christos, is sometimes used without the article to signify the one who, by His Holy Spirit and power, indwells believers and molds their character in conformity to His likeness.

"To them God has chosen to make known among the Gentiles the glorious riches of this mystery, which is Christ in you, the hope of glory (Col. 1:27)." The biographer, playwright, screenwriter, and script writer; Jesus of Nazareth has taken habitation inside of them.

The moment that you decided to accept Christ as your Lord and Personal Savior, He claimed you as His own. Yes, even if it was just a few seconds, minutes, hours, or days. Jesus is in you, and He will be from now on.

Prayer: Thank you Jesus for dwelling in me. We must continue in it every day for, the moment that we stop moving closer to Jesus, there is a possibility that we will go back to the way we were in the Word.

You see, here in this natural world, you are surrounded by ungodliness; you live in a body that is totally natural, unless you purposely counter that with daily prayer and spend time in the Word. Your body and mind will simply give into the pleasures around you if you and you will fall away from the Creator if you do not remain connected to Him through his prayer and following His Word.

Day 2

Get Closer To God

John 15:5

"I am the vine; you are the branches if you remain in me, and I in you, you will bear much fruit; apart from me you can do nothing."

Abiding in Jesus is a lifestyle that involves discipline and effort.

We have to choose to give ourselves in our union with Him and to give Him first place where our attention is concerned. If we want to grow spiritually, if we want to walk in power and in fellowship with the Lord, then we will have to spend the time it takes to know God. That is not something that we can do for a while and then move on to worldly things.

Prayer: The Holy Spirit helps me to be passionate about the word of God and to focus on the Lord daily in Jesus' name.

Day 3

Called and Chosen by God

Romans 8:28b

"Who have been called according to His purpose."

"And those He predestined, He also called those He called, He also justified; those He justified he also glorified (Rom. 8:30)."

Called means summoned or invited. It's used particularly in the divine call to partake of the blessings of redemption.

The word chosen also means elect/election. It's an expression of the Eternal, Sovereign will of God who cannot change, therefore the salvation of the elect is certain.

The characteristics of those that are called and chosen by God are that they love God, they are crazy about Him, and about the things of God.

Your Heavenly Father loves you unconditionally; so, don't be troubled by the things that are going on around you. The one who called you and chose you never changed. Those that are called by God are always known by Him. People may not be noticing you, but God knows every little detail about your life. When you know that you are chosen by God, it gives you confidence you would only know from the Father. Someone who has been called by God into a healing ministry, in time, must learn that it is not his or her ability, but the One who chose them for this task. Now, though it still requires faith to function at that level, it is not the same as someone who just want to heal people. Yes, as believers, we all can pray for the sick and they will recover like Jesus promised, but someone who operates daily with the gift of healing is not the same as us who pray for the sick. That individual was set a part specifically to pray for the sick and to ask Jesus for His love and mercy.

Day 4

The Blessings of Those That Are Called By God

Romans 8:30

"And those He predestined, He also called, those He called, He also justified: Those He justified, He also glorified."

He justified them. Justification is God's declaration that the demand of His law has been fulfilled in the righteousness of His Son. The basis for this justification is the death of Christ. When God justified, He charged the sins of mankind to Christ and credited the righteousness of Christ to the believer. Because of His justification, you have been declared not guilty, no matter where you have been or what you have done, because you have been called and chosen by God. In Christ you have been declared not guilty. There is no longer any fear for us believers. Although the Lord Jesus Christ has paid the price for our justification, it is through our faith that He is received, and His righteousness is experienced and enjoyed.

I believe that the most rewarding thing about being chosen by God is when God Himself rewards us in heaven. Each time the gift is in operation, and someone gets set free by our ministry, we experience joy, peace, and love. The angels could have done a better and faster job than us, but God chose us humans as his preference to advance his Kingdom.

Day 5

Christ Glorify God, God Glorify Christ, And God Will Glorify Us.

Romans 8:30B

"The word glorify means to magnify God through praising His name and Honoring His commands. Jesus also glorified His Father through His perfect obedience and His sacrificial death on our behalf."

God manifests all His goodness in the Son by glorifying Him. When Christ returns, He will glorify us by restoring our body parts. We will have a new body and we will look like God.

Our suffering now can't compare to the glory
that is waiting for us in Heaven.

Day 6

Spark Off On Purpose

1 Sam 1:4-15

God is about to turn things around, but the people in your life who are used to your daily routine might not even be aware of it.

God is about to do something extraordinary in your life.

Hannah didn't recognize who she was, but God used the other wife to push her into a purpose to receive her miracle baby.

God also used the priest Eli's wrongful thinking and words for her purpose.

Her answer to the priest changed the course of her household and Hannah said "not so my Lord. I am a woman who is deeply troubled." She had not been drinking wine or beer. was pouring out her soul to the Lord; that provoked the priest to bless her, and God answered her prayers that day.

Day 7

Prosperity In Every Area Of Your Life.

Proverbs 14:11

"The House of the wicked will be destroyed,
but the tent of the upright will flourish."

The Lord really cares about your finances
and about every need in your life.

Prosperity is a part of salvation. Some people think that being saved means you have to be poor; it is just the opposite of that. Your lives will flourish because you are righteous in the sight of God.

There is no lack in the house of the righteous.
We prosper with God's blessings.
Prosperity is the result of obeying God, and it comes when we apply God's Word (Law) abundantly in our lives.

The results come when we do it right. Give it to the Lord instead of a minister or ministry even when it hurts;
we must use our faith when we do it.

Prayer: Lord, I believe in you for every need that I have in my life in Jesus' name. My God shall supply all my needs according to His riches and glory by Christ Jesus.

Day 8

The God Who Opens Door

Isaiah 22:22

"Then I will set the key of the house of David on His shoulder, when He opens no one will shut. When He shuts no one will open."

You have to remind yourself who your doorkeeper is. You have to keep these scriptures in your mind that God will open the doors that no person can shut.

The enemy may have put you behind a door of sickness, poverty, disaster, or a door of trouble and addictions. You may feel trapped and that there is no way out. God wouldn't have let that door close if He didn't have a way to open it.

God is your door keeper. He is in control of your destiny. God is about to open the doors that have been shut for you for years.

You are about to walk in the things that you have been shut out of; the right people, promotion, abundance, healing, victory is coming your way.

Day 9

Play To Win

1 John 5:5

"Who is it that overcomes the world?
Only the one who believes that Jesus is the son of God."

If you play the game right, you will win.

Any coach will tell you that part of playing the game right is having a winning attitude. That is what God wants for you as a believer too. He wants us to have so much faith in Him that we expect to beat any obstacle the devil brings our way. He wants us to expect to win at the game of life, but most of us don't come by that attitude easily. We are so accustomed to losing that we have totally changed our way of thinking if we want to have a winning mindset. In the book of Ephesians, the apostle Paul told the church to renew their mind because, like us, they needed to change their attitudes and to renew their minds to the fact that Jesus overcame the world. If you haven't already, you need to do that too. You need to develop a glorious sense of confidence that says, "Hey devil, I am going to be victorious and there is not a thing that you can do to stop me."

Day 10

Choose To Be Happy

Psalm 118:24

"The Lord has done it this very day; Let us rejoice today and be glad."

If you are going to be happy, you have to be happy on purpose because there will always be challenging situations in your life like people betraying you; with all kinds of things that can make you bitter, sorrowful. You have to put your foot down and decide that you will not let these awful things in life make you unhappy.

When you wake up in the morning, put a command in your day. Be the prophet in your own life by using the Word of God as your guidance to be happy and victorious. Dictate the days, months, and years to come. Remember King David: he chose to encourage himself in the Lord.

Day 11

2 Timothy 1:7

"For God hath not given us the spirit of fear,
but of power and of love and of a sound mind."

God created everything else before he created man, yet he gave them authority; dominion over everything. You may be wondering, 'did God gave me dominion over snakes, the most dangerous animals?' The answer is yes. Now these are visibly terrifying things that you see, yet your Heavenly Father gave you power over all these deadly creatures. Fear is not just a reaction to your past, current, nor future circumstances. It is a spiritual force. It begins inside of you. That is why it is Satan's number one weapon against God 's children. Today, you should close that entrance door to the devil in your life by opening the door of power and might that God had created you to be. You have His abilities. Fight the good fight of faith.

Day 12

Your Thoughts Have The Power To Transform Your Life and Give You A Better Future.

Psalm 37:1-3

"Trust in the Lord and do good dwell in the land and feed on his faithfulness.

The Lord himself says as a man thinks so is he."

Think in the old testament means Chashab: to think, devise, purpose, esteem, count, and imagine. In Gen 38: 15, Eli thought Hannah was drunk. Chashab cunning (This meaning of Chashab as cunning appears eleven times in Exodus), but this skill was more than human invention; it indicated how the Spirit of God imparts wisdom, understanding, and knowledge. Feed your mind the right way daily by meditating with the Word of God; think positive. The flesh is weak, but the Spirit is willing. Visualize your future like Joshua and Caleb did when they had to enter, to possess, the promised land. Think of good things for your life: your spouse, your children, family, community, and nations. See yourself as a blessing to others: a curse breaker, and a victorious person that heals, delivers, prospers, and overcomes. When you begin to think like God, you will see, speak, and get things into existence.

Day 13

Be Loyal

1 Samuel 2: 30

"Therefore the Lord, the God of Israel, declares: I promised that members of your family would minister before me forever, but now the Lord declares far be it from me! Those who honor me, I will honor, but those who despise me will be disdained."

When you make the Lord your God your first choice by honoring him with your life and your lips, then you are stepping into a realm of blessing that will take an eternity to fully apprehend, comprehend, discover, and explore. Once you begin to get that kind of eternal perspective on things, you will bless the Lord at all times; his praise shall continually be in your mouth when things don't work out exactly how or when you want them too. You will see that your loyalty must be first of all to God. Just as it says in the book of Matthew, you must seek first the kingdom of God and His righteousness when things seem to be going wrong. God will never forget that, when you were going through hardship, you still decided to honor Him and speak of His promises.

Day 14

Divine Protection

Psalm 91

"Whoever dwells in the secret place of the most High
will rest in the shadow of the Almighty."

To be in an intimate place of divine protection is to spend quality time admiring the Lord in His presence: to give Him affection, to care for Him as you cast all your care, to give your worry to Him. It is not a relationship of what the Lord can do for you. There is much more to it and the time you spend with him will reveal this to you. Indeed, being at that level with the Lord, there is divine protection and provisions. The use of the most High for God emphasizes that no threat, no harm, can overpower him. "Shadow of the Almighty in a land where the sun can be oppressive and dangerous, a shadow was understood as a metaphor for care and protection (Psalm 91)."

Think about how much the devil hates people and how devoted he is to destroy them. It is no wonder we see so much tragedy and disaster in the world. In fact, it is amazing that we don't see more. The devil can't just come in to destroy if we, as God's people, don't give him access to certain things. If he could, he would have killed every human that God ever created; knocked every plane out of the sky and every boat on the sea, but he can't do it. Why? Because he is bound and limited. He has to line up certain things in the natural, human realm before he can lay a finger on you. He has to use people as his vessels or puppets to get his work or message across. The devil can't cause disaster in your life unless he has been given a place to. He can't come in and start destroying and stealing from you unless he can get you into a place of sin, doubt, ignorance, or disobedience. Remember the Israelites from the Old Testament. No army can defeat them whenever they obey God. Every time they turned their back on the Lord, He let the enemies won the battle on purpose until they could admit their wrong, turn their faces toward God and repent. Joshua had to ask God why they lost the fight. So, if the devil is giving you trouble, ask the Holy Spirit to show you how you let the evil one in. Then repent and get rid of him.

Day 15

Reaching and Touching The Invisible

It begins with faith.

Faith dwells in the unseen world, in the supernatural realm.

HebrewsS 11: 1

"Now faith is the confidence in what we hope for and assurance about what we do not see. There is no past, no future in faith cause faith is now."

The faith described here involves the most solid, possible conviction. The God given present assurance of a future reality, evidence of things not seen, true faith is not based on empirical evidence, but on divine assurance and is a gift from God.
Only by faith can we praise the Lord; only by faith
can we give to the Lord like Abel did.

Faith declared us righteous. It can translate us from one world to another. Faith enables us to come to God. It also rewards us.

Day 16

Endurance

How do we endure, stay strong, in the face of adversity?

Philippians 4:13

"I can do all things through Christ who gives me strength."

In the passage refered to above, Paul uses a Greek verb that means to be strong or to have strength. He had strength to withstand all things, including both difficulty and prosperity in the material world. The Greek word for strengthens means to put power in because believers are in Christ. He infuses them with His strength to sustain them until they receive some provision. I don't trust myself to start and finish well. My dependance is on the Lord. A lot of people in the Bible, and in the world that we live in now, started well and finished bad like Saul and Samson. However, Samson cried out to the Lord for help so that he would not finish the same way as the enemy. So how exactly do we stay focused and strong in the Lord?

We have to work in the light, work in the present truth and not in the past. We can't survive in the future if we are still working in the past. God requires for us to work in greater light and revelation; not dwelling in the past. Renewing the mind is not a one-time experience; it's done day by day. Renewing the old man keeps the faith day by day. We must look at Jesus as our example. Jesus, being full of the Spirit of God, was led into the wilderness. If we are full of the Holy Spirit remaining in Him, then we will never lack anything. Jesus was tempted in every form for forty days yet overcame every temptation. He returned in the form of the power of the Holy Ghost in Jerusalem. So, it is possible for us to remain strong after we have gone through temptations and trials.

Day 17

The Living Word Our Guide, Our Judges

Hebrews 4:12

"For the word of God is alive and active. Sharper than any double-edged sword, it penetrates even to divide soul and Spirit, joints and marrow, it judges the thought and attitudes of the heart."

While the word of God is comforting and nourishing to those who believe, it is a tool of judgment and execution for those who have not committed themselves to Jesus Christ. Some of the Hebrews were merely going through the motions of belonging to Christ intellectually; they were at least partly persuaded, but inside they were not committed to him. God's word would expose their shallow beliefs and their false intention. I recently had a decision to make about a television program which was offered to me for a little amount of money along with a few other things that I wanted to do for the kingdom of God. Deep down inside, however, I knew that no one knows me better than my maker so I took this verse, and I began to chew on it; ponder, and prayed with it so that the Holy Spirit can reveal to me the real motives of my heart. Was it about to show people that all is well, that I am more than able, capable of doing things or was it really about advancing, promoting the kingdom of God? As it turned out, the tv programming was not what I thought it would be at the end, and I realized that it was not God's timing for me. I am so glad that I took the time to ask God. My heart was in the right place, but the offer was not a good deal after all. Praise the Lord.

Day 18

Don't Determine To Stay In A Place of Complacency

Proverbs 13:4

"The soul of the sluggard craves and gets nothing,
while the soul of the diligent is richly supplied."

Complacency is a feeling of quiet pleasure or security, often while unaware of potential danger, defect, self-satisfaction, or smug satisfaction with an existing situation, or condition, Etc.

Just being content in our lives is what makes it bad because when we are satisfied with less than what God has for us. There is a difference between trusting God after you have done your best and settling in for less than what God has for you. Realize today that you need to stop and take a breather to appreciate yourself for the little things that you have accomplished. Clap for yourself for your success. It makes you human and it's more than okay to do so; just don't settle there and keep climbing the ladder. God has more in store for you. In Genesis, everything that God created, He said that it was good. He clapped for himself. Praise God for all the baby steps that you made, celebrate yourself in the process, and just don't settle for less.

Day 19

When You Uncertain About What To Do

Mark 5: 35-36

"While Jesus was still speaking, some people came from the house of Jairus, the Synagogue leader. Your daughter is dead, they said. "Why bother the teacher anymore?" Overhearing what they said, Jesus told him. "Don't be afraid, just believe."

Excessive talking about the wrong thing is possibly one of our biggest problems.

To talk about it too much means that you are giving it priority. You are focusing on it. The more you try to solve the mystery by focusing on it, the bigger it becomes. This is the perfect example on how to handle a situation. When Jairus' daughter got sick, he came to Jesus for help. He simply asked him to cure his daughter and took a risk that most people would not dare too. He visualized the solution instead of the problem by thinking about it and trying to cure a disease; an illness that has no cure can make you extremely fatigued. He decided to surrender to Jesus instead of complaining about it. Jesus was always and is still willing to help anybody who needs help, so he went with Jairus. While they were on their way, some people came with the bad news. It is too late, don't bother the teacher for the child's death. Jesus overheard and ignored them. Jesus said to the ruler of the synagogue. "Don't worry, keep on believing."

Day 20

Experience Abundant In Difficult Time

Matthew 6: 22

"The eyes are the lamp of the body. If your eyes are healthy your whole body will be full of light."

May the Lord anoint your eyes so you might see beyond the natural. When people see nature, they can't be blessed. It is time you see things like God sees it. Don't allow unbelief or doubt to rob you of your promises of God. God is on your side so all is well. Remember Isaac; he prospered in a time of famine. I declare today, over your life during famine and destruction, you will have the God kind of faith more than enough. God has made a covenant with you that can't be broken. The only thing that can break it is fear. You have to rely on the blessings of God. It makes one rich and adds no sorrow to it. We have to act by faith and take God at His work.

An example of experiancing abundance in a diffcult time would be during a time when there was a young preacher who just started preaching and he asked God for a desk, a chair, and a computer. The next day he decided to testify about having all these three things by faith. Since most people knew that he was really poor, a group of them followed him home to confirm what he just said. When they arrived at his place, he had none of what he said so they asked him why he deceived them. He replied that last night, in prayer, when he asked God for these things, at the moment, he had them insdie him. So, he choose to thank God for them publicly. They all laughed. Amazingly, three months later, God supernaturally gave him what he asked for and the whole town witnessed it.

Day 21

Lord Have Mercy On Me. Transform My Life

Proverb 12: 1

"Whoever loves discipline loves knowledge,
but whoever hates correction is stupid."

A variety of individuals, especially Christians don't know how to receive corrections without letting it condemn them.

The only way that we can grow up is through correction. That's how God helps us to become mature Christians. God only corrects those whom he loves. We don't like taking things from our children that we know it's going to wound them emotionally, but we do it because we want them to have a better and brighter future. Sometimes we do it for different reasons when, in reality, we love them, but when God tries to remodel us if our response to that is condemnation. Then we don't receive what God is trying to do and we have to go to the same situations as the Israelite in the wilderness for forty years instead of forty days. A spiritually mature Christian can actually be grateful when God shows them something is wrong in their lives because they are quick to repent and ask the Holy Spirit to help and guide them to correct the problem. They are overcomers; they receive all that God has for them by letting Him lead the way. If you know who you are in Christ and understand the blood of Jesus, then you know that God's love for you is eternal; it is a sure thing then and there is no reason to feel condemned when he rebukes you. All your Heavenly Father wants you to do is agree with him. Yes God, I have a problem changing me. It is not that I have already obtained all this or have already arrived at my goal, but I press on to take hold of that for which Christ Jesus took hold of me. It's going to take forever to be loved if you condemn yourself; let go and the power of the Holy Spirit changes you. It is possible.

Day 22

Your Words Become Your Reality

Proverb 18:21

The tongue has the power of life and death and those who love it will eat its fruit "And the Lord saith to Moses I would do what you say, because you have found mercy in my sight (Prov. 18:21)." You are who you are and where you are today because of what you have been spoken about. If you continue to say it, then it will come to pass. Whenever you speak, you are prophesying your future. You are planting seeds when you talk, and you are going to reap the fruits from the words that come out of your mouth. If you don't like what you see, change your words by speaking words of life, success, favor, healing, and new opportunity instead. What if today is the day that God tells you that He will do exactly what He hears you whisper in His ears. Think about it for a moment, what would you do? What could you speak into existence at this very moment with your words? You can bless and you can curse your future. Reverse the chaos in your life and choose blessings by confessing it instead; bless the nations. Call things that are not there as though they were. Glory to God

Day 23

Suffering

James 1:2

"Consider it pure joy, my brothers and sisters, whenever you face trials of many kinds because you know that the testing of your faith produces perseverance, let perseverance finish its work so that you may be mature and complete, not lacking anything."

People don't like suffering ot the mentioning of it. So, we often give it another name because we don't like the package that comes with it. Suffering means to live or to permit, to bear with or stay under it as humans. The first thing that we want to do when we suffer is to run, but you have to go through the hard part to get to the good part. God makes all things beautiful in his timing. Your maker always makes the wrong thing right if we trust Him and if we handle the wrong thing in the right way. A positive way. He is always fair.

Day 24

Victory Begins In The Dark

1 John 5: 4-5

"For everyone born of God overcomes the world.
This is the victory that has overcome the world, even our faith.
Who is it that overcomes the world? Only the one who
believes that Jesus is the Son of God."

Don't go by your feelings or by your emotions because they don't always tell you the truth. The book of Genesis begins with the dark; that is where God started. God didn't start the day with the light for a purpose. It is symbolic for how he does things in our lives. You can't see it, but you have to believe it. Walk by faith, not by sight. All things are possible for those that believe. You also have to remember what is impossible with men is indeed possible with God. At the end of the tunnel there will be light.

When you have been at your best and nothing is changing, then you have to know that light is coming. You must not get discouraged, instead praise him in the middle of the uncertainty. It may look too big or impossible for you, but God is not through with you. He will do something out of the extraordinary to bring you victory. He is not done with you.

Day 25

Desperate Faith

Matthew 15: 21-28

This woman was not a follower of Jesus, she was an observer. She was desperate enough to cross her line of tradition; she was not Jewish. According to Hebrew 11:1, Now faith is the confidence in what we hope for and assurance about what we do not see. And, without faith, it is impossible to please God because anyone who comes to him must believe that he exists and that he rewards those who earnestly seek him. Sometimes we blame God for our own mistakes; so, we must first admit that we got ourselves in trouble. Faith without works is dead; so, go out there by faith and make it happen. This woman used her faith and got on God's agenda. Desperate faith does not reject God's decision or will. You still have to find out what the Lord is doing in the season that you are in and trust that He will get you through it. It is not witchcraft. The thing that made this woman desperate was that she had a devil to fight. Today, do what it takes to get the devil out of your mind, your soul, your children, your marriage, your family etc.

Day 26

Facing Your Fears

Isaiah 41:10

"So do not fear, for I am with you; do not be dismayed,
for I am your God. I will strengthen you and help you."

The truth is that fear is a part of our lives. When the Bible says fear not, It does not mean that you won't feel fear. It means that when you feel fear, keep doing what God asked you to do, and to keep moving forward by doing what you suppose to do. Fear prevents forward progress and keeps you from doing what you were called to do. Confrontation is something that most people hate in their lives, but it is something that you should value. God does not always take us the easy way out. Sometimes you have to remind yourself that God is still in complete control.

Day 27

How To Hear The Voice of God

John 10:27

"My sheep listen to my voice: I know them, and they follow me."

Your spirit can be educated just like your mind can be. You can build yourself up spiritually to hear from God. 1) By meditation of the word of God. 2) By practicing the word of God. 3) By praising God. Praises remove all ear blog; God inhabits the praise of his people.

We are to hear God's voice not the devil. When we don't hear His voice, we sin. Incline your ear to Him, come to Him, and He will make an everlasting covenant with you. You have to exercise your hearing abilities, in both your senses and spirituality. People who are not accustomed to God's voice will not hear him. Ever heard of the term that practice makes perfect? Without it,
we can't discern from both good and evil.

Day 28

Keys To Hear The Voice of God

Isaiah 30: 15-21

Verse 18 Yet the Lord longs to be gracious to you; Therefore, He will rise up to show you compassion. Blessed are all who wait for him.

Verse 20-21 Although the Lord gives you the bread of adversity and the water of affliction, your teachers will be hidden no more with your own eyes, you will see them. Whether you turn to the right or the left, your ears will hear a voice behind you saying,
"This is the way walk in it."

Key# 1:

Withdraw from all worldly distractions, all problems, if you speak to someone before talking to God, it will block you from hearing clearly. When you wake up in the morning,
you should talk to God first.

Day 29

The Second Key to Hearing God's Voice

Jeremiah 33:3

"Call to me and I will answer you, and will tell you great and hidden things that you have not known."

The second key to hearing God's voice.

Turn off your phones, shout out all noise. Let God *hear* your voice talking to Him. Jesus prayed while He was getting baptism then the heaven opened up and God spoke to Him in the book of Matthew.

Key# 3: God speaks to those who seek His will.

Key# 4: Those who tremble at His Word and those who are broken: He will not speak if you have pride in your heart.

Key# 5: When you don't hear God *read* Him by reading the word that is also God speaking to you.

Day 30

How To Have Full Joy

The believer, who is mainly in a healthy spiritual state of mind, rejoices daily regardless of what is going on in their lives.

1 John 1:4

"We write this to make our joy complete."

The Lord exalts His people to rejoice always. Although your problems, your afflictions, troubles, and sorrows are in this world, joy is *not* in this world. The joy of the Lord is the strength of His people. Such strength always reveals itself practically when trouble comes, and your faith is in trials. It has been tested. The proof of our faith may not overlook the priceless virtue that is produced by this process. We shall know the spiritual completeness. Joy is brought to our door, by the love of God and all the attributes of God become joy.

We shall know the spiritual completeness. By Charles Spurgeon

Day 31

Let Healing Flow

Mark 16:17-18

"And these signs will accompany those who believe in my name they will drive out demons; They will speak in tongues. They will pick up snakes with their hands and when they drink deadly poison it will not hurt them at all; they will place their hands on sick people, and they will get well."

Rapha: "Restoring to normal an act with God typically performs. A large number of the uses of Rapha express the healing "as a figure of the act of God's grace and forgiveness, as well as the nation's repentance.

Sozo: "to save", is translated by the verb to heal and to make whole. The idea is that of saving from disease and its effects.

Healing is a part of the gospel.

Healing is yours today, open your heart to receive it in Jesus' name.

Day 32

Miracles

Mark 16: 15-20

"He said to them, "Go into all the world and preach the gospel to all creation. Whoever believes and is baptized will be saved, but whoever does not believe will be condemned. And these signs will accompany those who believe: In my name they will drive out demons; they will speak in new tongues; they will pick up snakes with their hands; and when they drink deadly poison, it will not hurt them at all; they will place their hands on sick people, and they will get well."

After the Lord Jesus had spoken to them, he was taken up into heaven and he sat at the right hand of God. Then the disciples went out and preached everywhere, and the Lord worked with them and confirmed his word by the signs that accompanied it."

Miracles are the supernatural act of God for the Christians. There are the manifestation of the power of God. It's the intervention of God in the life of the believer. Miracles happen to help people to believe. Today when you doubt that miracles don't exist it's like saying God doesn't exist because when it take place God makes it happen and miracles show how big our God is. The will of God is to bless his children. So, receive your miracles today in Jesus name whatever the need is.

Day 33

Healing Part 2

God anointed Jesus the Nazareth who went about doing good.

If you believe that sickness comes from God, then you can't receive healing nor pray for the sick. The only way you can operate in divine healing is by following the wind of the Spirit and God will lead you there. If you are in doubt about the will of God for your life, then just look at Jesus. He is the perfect example. The sacrificial Lamb for our healings. Jesus is the will of God in action.

Satan is behind your problems and your diseases,
but God promised to heal his people.

God is in the healing business, not the sickness one.
Jesus heals all the oppress of the devil.

Be healed in Jesus' name and by His stripes you were healed.

Day 34

Redeemed From The Curse of The Law

Galatians 3: 13

"Christ redeemed us from the curse of the Law by becoming a curse for us, for it is written: cursed is everyone who is hung on a pole"

To be Redeem means to be spared from God's wrath and judgment; to be set free from its rule and regulations. We no longer have to pay for our sins because Christ paid the penalty for us.

Ga'al–Verbs

"To redeem, deliver, avenge, act as kinsman". This word's basic use had to do with the deliverance of a person or property that had been sold for debt.

Padah: "To redeem, ransom." Padah indicates that some intervening, or substitutionary action affects a release from an undesirable condition from death.

Day 35

The Miraculous Realm of The Spirit

Every prophecy that was written before Jesus' time was in the miracle realm. His incarnation was a real miracle. He was not born under the natural laws of generation. He was conceived of the Holy Ghost. He was a true incarnation, God uniting himself with humanity, the scenes surrounding his birth. The angelic visitation, the coming of the wise men all were miracles. The angels warning Joseph to flee with the child to Egypt was miraculous. The descent of the Spirit at his baptism was a miracle. From that day until Mount Olives was a period of miracles. His life among men was a miracle. The new kind of life that He revealed to the world was a miracle.

By John G Lake

Day 36

Different Kind of Prayers

Prayer is a two-way communication between God and you.

1) Prayer of petition; Prayer of faith. Whatever you ask, when you pray, believe that you receive it. (Matt. 21:22). Prayer of petition is praying for yourself. You can't receive for others, except parents for their children. If you don't know, it is God's will. You can't receive it by faith. You can't pray a prayer of faith that you are not sure of. Faith is the ground substructure (Rom. 8: 34). If you are hoping for something that you can see, then it is not hope because you can see it. Faith gives you proof of what you are not seen to receive. Matthew 13 is a parable of the word of faith. For those of you who are in ministry and feel guilty every time that you take time to pray for yourself; this is my way of telling you that you matter to God. Remember that it is more than okay to pray for yourself and ask your loving Father for great things.

Day 37

2) The Prayer of Consecration

Matthew 10:38

Whoever does not take up their cross and follow me
is not worthy of me.

It is not always convenient or perfect to do the will of God. If you don't obey God, you won't see his glory. In Luke 22: 42, Jesus is in the garden praying. All the disciples entered into temptation because they fell asleep, and they didn't pray like Jesus asked them to Jesus prayed so that he didn't enter into temptation and so that he didn't call the angels. He was tempted at every level and every area, and he overcame them because he prayed.

Prayer of Consecration

NOT MY WILL, BUT YOUR WILL.

Day 38

United Prayer

Act 4: 23-31

3) Praying in one accord. The disciples were in prison; everyone gathered together to pray out loud, lifting their voices to the Lord. They all were declaring the same thing.

The fruit of it—Results, powerful results, miracles and wonders took place.

DAY 38

THE PRAYER OF THANKSGIVING, PRAISE AND WORSHIP

PSALM 148

Praise shouted in the mouth of the enemy (Ps 8:2).

Thanksgiving and praise will keep you focused on the promises of God, not the problem. God inhabits the praises of his people. Your praise, your gratitude, in the mist of what you are going through, gives God a way to come into our problem and fight our battle. Thanksgiving and praise release your blessings that God has for you. Every time you praise in the spiritual realm you are clothed. Praise is a garment and an antidote for depression. It prepares the way for supernatural intervention.

Worship is ministering unto the Lord. It glorifies God focusing on who God is instead of what you can get. It is, in fact, the greatest way to receive from the Lord.

Day 39

Ways To Increasing God's Favor In Your Life

Luke 2: 52

"And Jesus increased in wisdom and stature, and in favor with God and man."

If you want the favor of God in your life, you have to change the way you live. A life that is pleasing unto the Lord. Analyze your way of doing things, both in the past and present. Your conduct and your actions have everything to do with whether or not you increase in the favor. Do a self-evaluation; the Bible mentioned to judge yourself so that others will not judge you. You must learn to practice the presence of God daily in prayer and by reading His Word.

When God speaks to you, be quick to obey. When the favor of God goes before you, it *will* enable you to take possession of what is rightfully yours.

Day 40

Benefits of The Favor of God

Genesis 39: 21

"But the Lord was with Joseph and showed him mercy and gave him favor in the sight of keepers of the prison."

1) Favor opens doors for supernatural increase and promotion in your life.

2) Favor creates a platform of recognition, even when you seem the least likely to receive it.

3) Favor makes you eat the good of the land and the best of it. It makes you the head and not the tail; above and not beneath.

4) Favor produces great wealth and increases in assets.

5) Favor goes first before giving you honor in the sight of your enemies.

Bibliography

Dr. Mireille Michel Simon sermons used with permission.

Greetings in the name of our Lord Jesus Christ! God's will is the Holy Spirit by Gloria Copeland. Kenneth Copeland publications. 1990 Eagle Mountains International Church Inc.

Walk in the Spirit by Gloria Copeland. Publisher Kenneth Copeland Ministries January 1, 1998,

John G Lakes, his life, his sermons, his boldness of faith by Kenneth Copeland. Vendor: Harrison House, publication date: 2013,

Charles Spurgeon. The selected Sermons of Charles Spurgeon volume 3 sermons and volume 4,

TD. Jakes Destiny- Step into your purpose. Vendor : Faith Words. Publication date: 2015,

few of my notes from Life Christian University,

Good Morning Holy Spirit by Benny Hinn. March 2004 Publisher: Thomas Nelson. And few of his sermons from BHI notes.

New International Version (NIV)
Holman Bible Publishers, November 1, 2016

KING JAMES version,

The message Bible,
Eugene H. Peterson, Navpress September 28, 2005

The Vines complete Expository Dictionary,
W.E. Vine, Merrill F. Unger, William White Jr., Thomas Nelson September 22, 1996

THE NEW STRONG'S CONCISE CONCORDANCE
James Strong, LL.D., S.T.D., Thomas Nelson 2005

VINE'S CONCISE DICTIONARY OF THE BIBLE.
W.E. Vine, Thomas Nelson June 19, 2005

Milton Keynes UK
Ingram Content Group UK Ltd.
UKHW041941090224
437558UK00001B/100